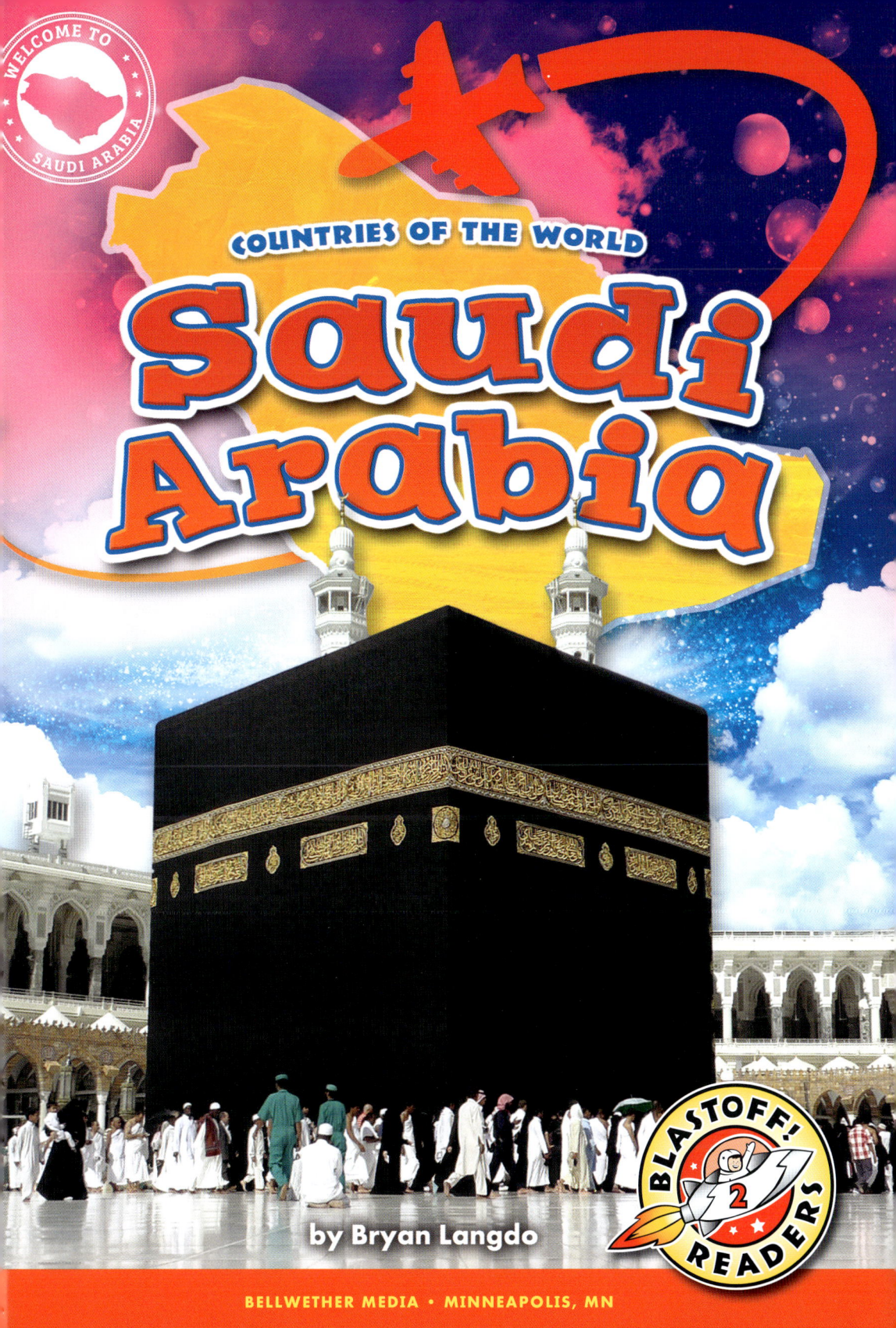

Blastoff! Readers are carefully developed by literacy experts to build reading stamina and move students toward fluency by combining standards-based content with developmentally appropriate text.

LEVELS

Level 1 provides the most support through repetition of high-frequency words, light text, predictable sentence patterns, and strong visual support.

Level 2 offers early readers a bit more challenge through varied sentences, increased text load, and text-supportive special features.

Level 3 advances early-fluent readers toward fluency through increased text load, less reliance on photos, advancing concepts, longer sentences, and more complex special features.

★ **Blastoff! Universe**

Reading Level

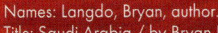

This edition first published in 2025 by Bellwether Media, Inc.

No part of this publication may be reproduced in whole or in part without written permission of the publisher. For information regarding permission, write to Bellwether Media, Inc., Attention: Permissions Department, 6012 Blue Circle Drive, Minnetonka, MN 55343.

Library of Congress Cataloging-in-Publication Data

Names: Langdo, Bryan, author.
Title: Saudi Arabia / by Bryan Langdo.
Description: Minneapolis, MN : Bellwether Media, Inc., 2025. | Series: Blastoff! readers. Countries of the world | Includes bibliographical references and index. | Audience: Ages 5-8 | Audience: Grades 2-3 | Summary: "Relevant images match informative text in this introduction to Saudi Arabia. Intended for students in kindergarten through third grade"– Provided by publisher.
Identifiers: LCCN 2024039284 (print) | LCCN 2024039285 (ebook) | ISBN 9798893042337 (library binding) | ISBN 9798893043303 (ebook)
Subjects: LCSH: Saudi Arabia–Juvenile literature.
Classification: LCC DS204.25 .L36 2025 (print) | LCC DS204.25 (ebook) | DDC 953.8–dc23/eng/20240923
LC record available at https://lccn.loc.gov/2024039284
LC ebook record available at https://lccn.loc.gov/2024039285

Text copyright © 2025 by Bellwether Media, Inc. BLASTOFF! READERS and associated logos are trademarks and/or registered trademarks of Bellwether Media, Inc.

Editor: Suzane Nguyen   Designer: Laura Sowers

Printed in the United States of America, North Mankato, MN.

Table of Contents

All About Saudi Arabia	4
Land and Animals	6
Life in Saudi Arabia	12
Saudi Arabia Facts	20
Glossary	22
To Learn More	23
Index	24

All About Saudi Arabia

Riyadh

Saudi Arabia is the biggest country in the **Middle East**. Its capital is Riyadh.

Islam started in Saudi Arabia. Nearly all Saudis practice Islam.

Land and Animals

The country is mostly flat **deserts**. The biggest desert is Rub' al-Khali.

Mountains rise in the southwest. The Red Sea lines the west. The Persian **Gulf** is to the east.

Red Sea

Rub' al-Khali

Size: around 250,000 square miles (647,497 square kilometers)

Famous For: the largest sand desert in the world

The country is **arid**. It is hot and dry most of the year.

The country gets very little rain. The air is cooler in the mountains.

Many animals live in the deserts.
Sand cats hunt for **prey**.
Camels travel far across the sands.

Arabian camel

Animals of Saudi Arabia

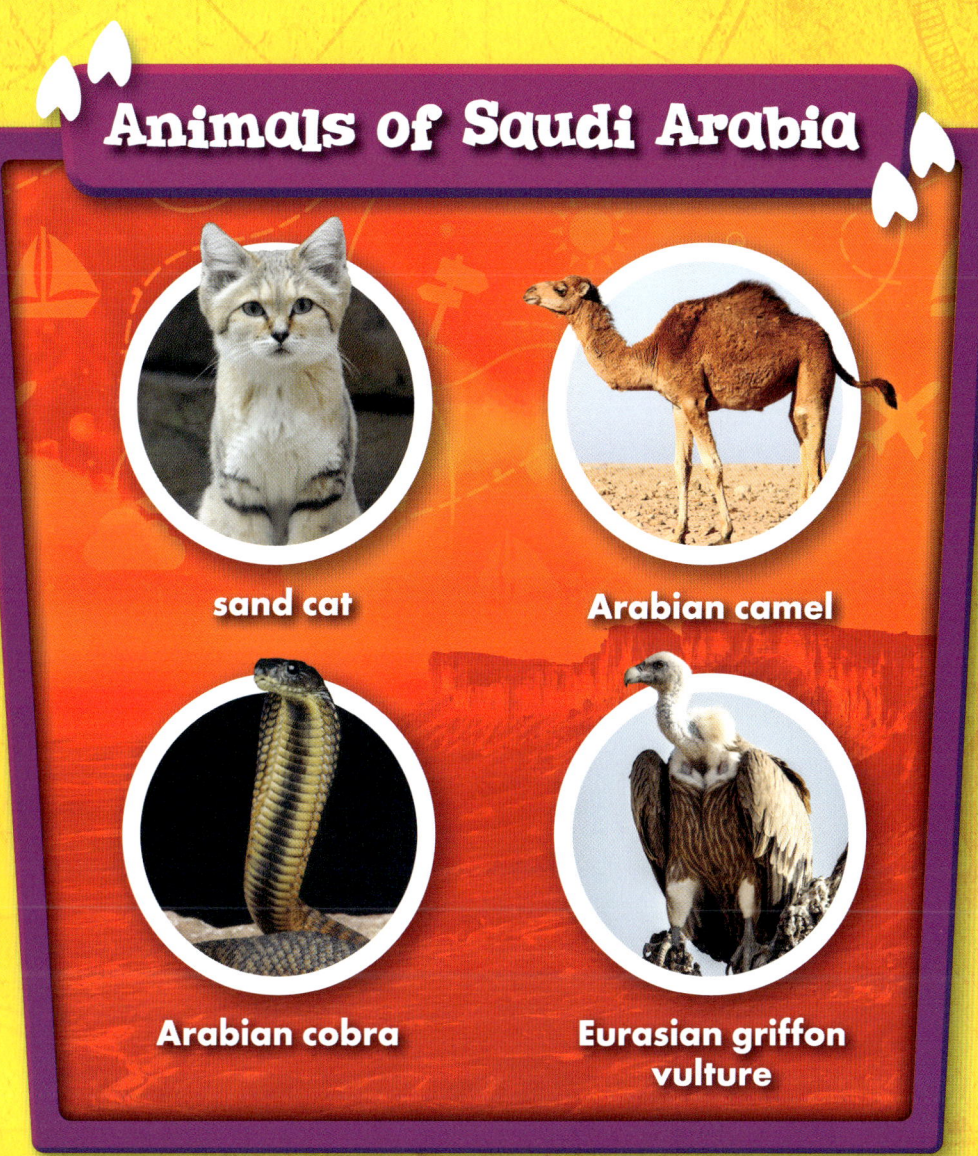

sand cat

Arabian camel

Arabian cobra

Eurasian griffon vulture

Cobras hide among rocks. Vultures fly high above.

Life in Saudi Arabia

Most Saudis are part of the Arab **ethnic** group. Arabic is mainly spoken.

Most people live in cities. The biggest city is Riyadh.

Saudis enjoy music, dance, and poetry. They also play video games.

Soccer is very popular. People also race camels and train falcons.

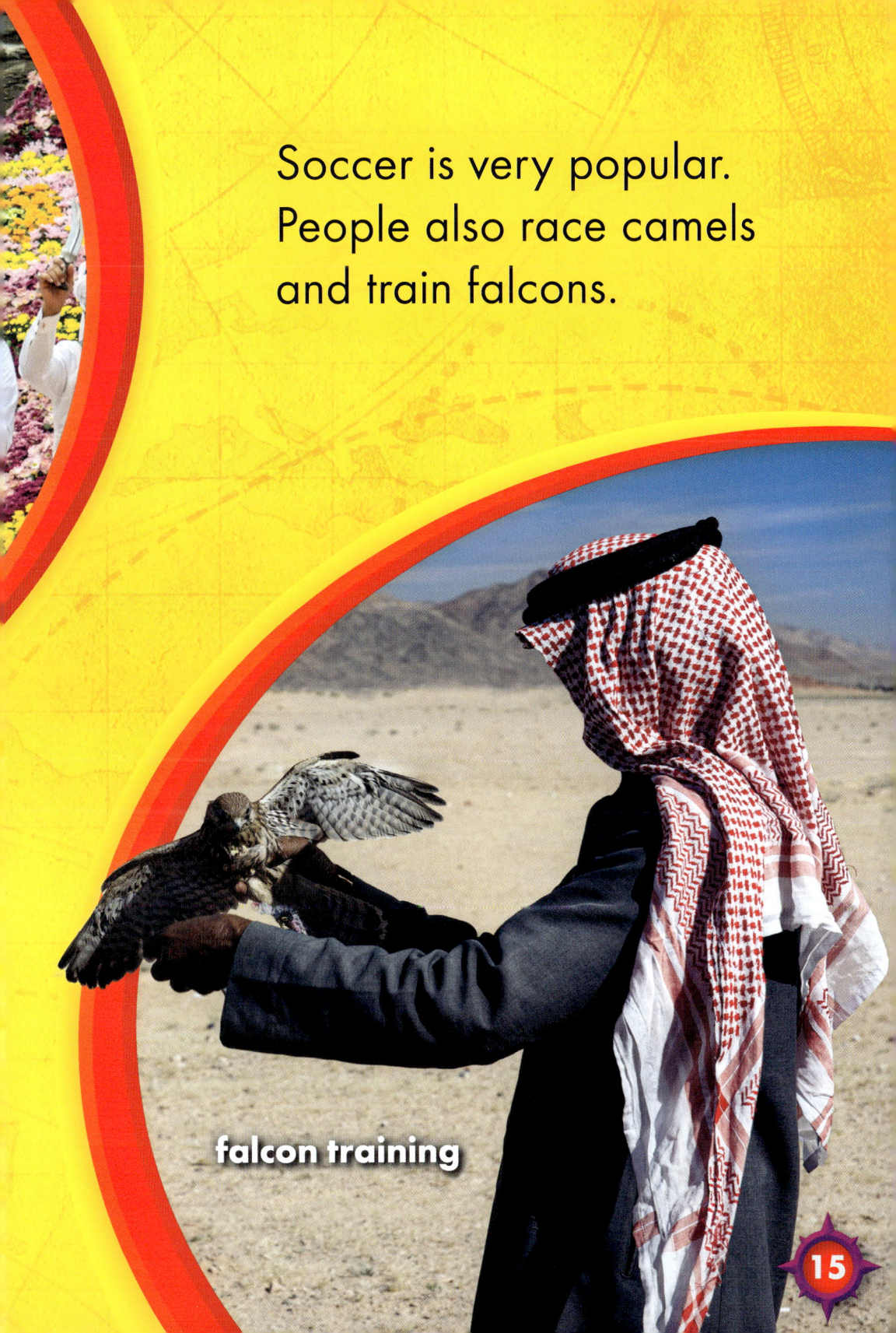

falcon training

Kabsa is a popular dish. It is rice with meat and spices. *Shawarma* is meat roasted on a stick.

Saudi Arabian Foods

kabsa

shawarma

falafel

dates

Falafel is made with chickpeas. Dates are a sweet fruit.

People pray and **fast** during Ramadan. This holiday lasts for a month. Then they share meals.

September 23 is Saudi National Day. Fireworks fill the sky! Saudis love their **culture**!

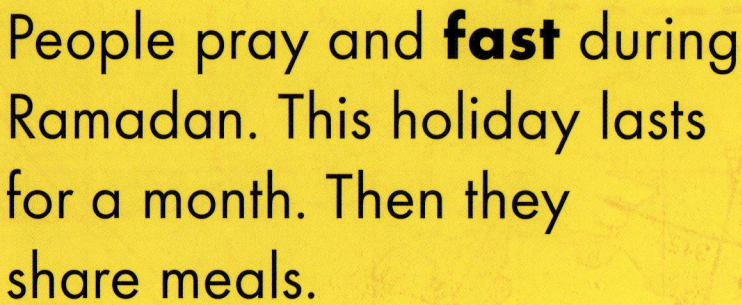

end of Ramadan

Saudi National Day

Saudi Arabia Facts

Size:
830,000 square miles
(2,149,690 square kilometers)

Population:
36,544,431 (2024)

National Holiday:
Saudi National Day (September 23)

Main Language:
Arabic

Capital City:
Riyadh

Famous Face

Name: Haifaa al-Mansour

Famous For: first female Saudi filmmaker

Religions

other: 3%

Muslim: 97%

Top Landmarks

Great Mosque of Mecca

Hegra

Prophet's Mosque

Glossary

arid—very dry, with little rainfall

culture—the beliefs, arts, and ways of life in a place or society

deserts—dry lands with few plants and little rainfall

ethnic—related to races or large groups of people who share things such as customs, religion, and language

fast—to stop eating all or some foods for a certain period of time

gulf—part of an ocean or sea extending into the land

Islam—a religion based on belief in Allah as the only God and in Prophet Muhammad as God's follower

Middle East—a region of southwestern Asia and northern Africa; the Middle East includes Egypt, Israel, Iran, Iraq, Lebanon, Saudi Arabia, Syria, and other nearly countries.

prey—animals that are hunted by other animals for food

To Learn More

AT THE LIBRARY
Crimeen, Carole, and Suzanne Fletcher. *Ramadan*. Minneapolis, Minn.: Lerner Publishing, 2023.

Gould, Sloane. *Saudi Arabia*. New York, N.Y.: Cavendish Square Publishing, 2024.

Spanier, Kristine. *Saudi Arabia*. Minneapolis, Minn.: Jump!, 2021.

ON THE WEB

FACTSURFER

Factsurfer.com gives you a safe, fun way to find more information.

1. Go to www.factsurfer.com.

2. Enter "Saudi Arabia" into the search box and click 🔍.

3. Select your book cover to see a list of related content.

Index

animals, 10, 11, 15
Arabic, 12
capital (see Riyadh)
culture, 18
dance, 14
deserts, 6, 10
falcon training, 15
food, 16, 17
Islam, 5
map, 5
Middle East, 4
mountains, 6, 9
music, 14
people, 5, 12, 14, 15, 18
Persian Gulf, 6
poetry, 14
rain, 9
Ramadan, 18
Red Sea, 6
Riyadh, 4, 5, 12

Rub' al-Khali, 6, 7
Saudi Arabia facts, 20–21
Saudi National Day, 18, 19
say hello, 13
soccer, 15
video games, 14

The images in this book are reproduced through the courtesy of: Sufi, front cover; Mini Onion, p. 3; t:mtcurado, pp. 4-5; Yousef Almulhim, p. 6; David Steele, pp. 6-7; Abdullah Aslshathri, pp. 8-9; Matthew Staring, p. 9; Guillaume Angleraud, pp. 10-11; PeteGallop, p. 11 (sand cat); Grego Nagy, p. 11 (Arabian camel); reptiles4all, p. 11 (Arabian cobra); Sourabh Bhurti, p. 11 (Eurasian griffon vulture); Mfee, p. 12; The Road Provides, pp. 12-13; Andrzej Lisowski Travel, p. 14; Muhammed Hamed Morsi, pp. 14-15; Nekrasov Eugene, p. 15; huzzein farar, p. 16 (*kabsa*); Vova Shevchuk, p. 16 (*shawarma*); Chzu, p. 16 (*falafel*); Photoongraphy, p. 16 (dates); Emily_M_Wilson, p. 17; xavierarnau, p. 18; AFZAL KHAN MAHEEN, pp. 18-19; Rena Joan, p. 20 (flag); Andrea Raffin, p. 20 (Haifaa al-Mansour); Mohamed Reedi, p. 21 (Great Mosque of Mecca); Vadim_N, p. 21 (Hegra); MoRdoi, p. 21 (Prophet's Mosque); Eric Isselee, p. 22.